BOOK SMACKDOWN

the ONE Thing you
Must Do to
Write Your Book
+ 10 EASY ways to
GET IT DONE!

TRACEE SIOUX

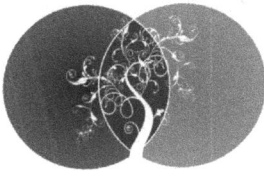

Sioux Ink

FORT COLLINS, COLORADO

Publishing House
Sioux Ink
BookSmackdown.com
traceesioux@gmail.com
Book Smackdown: the ONE thing you must do to Write your book + 10 EASY ways to GET IT DONE! / Tracee Sioux -- 1st edition.
ISBN-13: 978-1-946317-05-6
ISBN-10: 1-946317-05-5

TOO BUSY TO WRITE?

Visit this link for an exclusive FREE Course.

https://mailchi.mp/traceesioux.com/time-joy-gasm

You can also find me on Facebook at www.facebook/traceesioux and www.facebook.com/Yes-TraceeSioux

DEDICATION

For those who have the balls
to WRITE the book within you.
(instead of just talking about it.)
May this book inspire you to be
the ballsy one!

CHAPTERS

If you want to be a writer, you must do two things above all others: read a lot and write a lot. There's no way around these two things that I'm aware of, no shortcut.
~Stephen King, On Writing

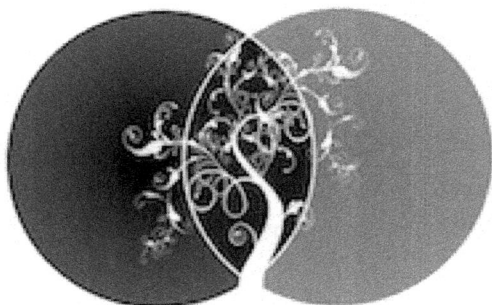

FOREWORD

You want to write a book.

This book lives in you.

It sucks up your mind-share. You think about it all the time. You worry it, it keeps you awake at night. It's there, in your New Year's Resolutions—year after year.

This book pesters you! It's constantly knocking on your brain ...

Why aren't you writing me? When is this going to get done? When will you have time to give me life?

By now it might be a heavy burden. You've disappointed yourself so many times. You keep thinking you'll do it next week or next month or next year. But you don't.

This leads to emotional creative blocks. Now you feel like you're a loser procrastinator who is unmotivated. You have this lingering sense that you're not a good enough writer.

These feelings of guilt and shame might even make you feel things like, "I hate writing."

Letting yourself down never feels good. It makes you feel like you're failing.

More terrifying to some is the potential outcome of actually putting your deepest thoughts out there for all to see ... criticize and review.

What if the Internet crucifies me? This is a legit fear that kept me from writing books. It is scary to put your words out into the ether where you don't have any control over how other people will perceive your book.

You're probably overwhelmed with the thought of it. Your life is full, your calendar is overflowing, you already have a plethora of responsibilities and writing a book seems like a daunting task.

This is never a great place to start the creative process.

In this book, *Book Smackdown: The ONE Single Thing You Must Do to Write Your Book*, I want to make the book-making process a clear and easy path.

First, I'm going to help you understand your own motivation for writing a book. What do you want from this?

Is this a childhood dream?

Is this a book that's going to launch your career into a whole new level?

Is this a legacy you want to leave your children and grandchildren?

Is this a story that won't leave your mind until you get it out?

Knowing your motivations will help you get into the space of writing a book with a clear intention. If you're writing to make yourself an expert or influencer in your profession you'll want to position the marketing of the book in line with your existing brand. But if you're writing a beautiful romance novel or a thriller you'll want to understand the different positioning required.

Then, I'm going to help you break through that overwhelm by dividing the book-making process into five distinct tasks rather than lumping the whole thing into "Write a Book."

You'll hear many writers describe the process of writing as "birthing a book." Birth is an exceptional metaphor for writing a book. There is a conception phase (the idea), a gestation period (allowing the idea to form within you), a labor process (putting the words on paper), a delivery phase (publishing the book and giving it life in the world as form) and then the phase that lasts 18 years, raising the kid (marketing the book).

As such, you might see me refer to each phase using the birth metaphor. Whether you're a man or a woman you should be able to relate to the concept.

These *5 Simple Steps to Writing a Book* include:

1. Research

2. Writing

3. Editing

4. Publishing

5. Marketing

Simply understanding the different processes that go into book-making can eliminate overwhelm; making you feel more confident and capable of getting this book finished.

The best part of understanding these steps as separate tasks is that YOU only have to do ONE of them. The *only* one you have to do is write that first draft. For all of the other parts you can (and SHOULD) hire a professional who specializes in the various functions. These professionals will take your book to the next level and make it much more likely that you'll be proud to put your name on it. If you're feeling confident about your book, you're not as afraid of what the Internet will say. You'll even be able to shake off criticism and the occasional book troll.

Then I'm going to give you 10 Easy Ways to Write Your Book. There is no right way or wrong way to write a book. Everyone has strengths and weaknesses when it comes to communication. There are ways to get that book on paper which will be effortless for you.

At the end of *Book Smackdown*, you'll have all the skills and information you need to birth that book into the world.

Writing a book should be so pleasurable that you want to do it again and again.

How will you feel when you get this big goal accomplished?

Proud. Excited. Competent. Relieved. Cathartic.

What's it worth to hold your book in your hand with your name on the cover?

It's so worth it. I promise.

Perfectionism is the voice of
the oppressor, the enemy of
the people. It will keep you
cramped and insane your
whole life, and it is the main
obstacle between you and a
shitty first draft.
~Anne Lamont,
Bird by Bird

MOTIVATION

There are several reasons a person is compelled to write a book. Let's go over a few of them and see which one resonates with you.

1. You're a **professional writer** and this is what you've always wanted to do with your life. You love the craft and creative energy that flows through you and you love seeing your name in the "by" line. You're establishing yourself as a legit writer/author; you're committed to your craft. Unfortunately, most people believe that this type of writer is the only kind that should be writing a book. Hogwash.

2. You want **professional credibility**. Writing a book about your chosen profession or field of study can launch your career to a whole new level. A book says to potential clients: I'm legitimate and credible; you can trust me. A book brings instant publicity, media, radio shows and speaking gigs. A book allows you to justify higher prices and fees. A book attracts a different breed of clientele.

3. You're a **hobby writer**. Writing brings you pleasure and allows you to get into the state of flow. It's something you do in your free time. Though it doesn't bring you money or success, you do it for the sheer joy it brings you. Oh yeah, this is one of the best feelings ever and that keeps you coming back.

4. You're a **purpose-driven writer**. For whatever reason your Soul or conscience is begging—even demanding—that you write this book. Maybe it's your job to record the family history, maybe it's a way to bring optimism, light and happiness to the world, perhaps your Soul wants to share its knowledge and wisdom. Whichever it is for you, it's driven by purpose.

Whatever your motivation for writing a book; it's awesome. Writing for any reason is a legitimate and valid thing to do.

Knowing your motivation for writing the book will help you position the book for sales, and marketing, guiding you during the writing process.

A book is the best
business investment
you'll ever make.
~Tracee Sioux, Sioux Ink

YOUR BOOK AS MARKETING

You may not make a single penny on your book. You might spend money and not make it back.

It's not impossible to make money on a book, but if that's your motivation—DON'T DO IT. You must do it for the sake of the journey.

There is an exception to this rule: use your book AS a marketing tool for your business.

If you own a business and you're trying to establish yourself as a credible expert in your field, a book is the best possible marketing you can have.

Let me explain why.

If you have a choice between two real estate agents and one of them has a FB page and a simple website, while the other has a published book providing great information, which would you choose?

If you have a choice between doctors, would you choose the one with a book over the one without a book?

Of course. A book is instant credibility.

Google Love

Just having a book on your website will give you better Google results if you use SEO correctly. When people visit your website they will see the book and believe you're more credible and knowledgable without any convincing on your part. They might even buy the book, which will lead to greater income.

Press and Media

A fantastic way to market your business is to be on podcasts, featured on websites, published in magazines and being interviewed for articles as *the expert* in your field.

The second you have a book it's almost too easy to garner media attention. As a journalist of 20 years, I know that journalists are constantly seeking more content and more knowledgable experts for quotes than they can find. They are looking for you!

You can sign up for simple email lists like Radio Guest List and Help a Reporter Out to look for opportunities to be interviewed. Now, who do you think the reporter or radio host is going to interview first—the professional with a book or the professional without?

Speaking Gigs

There are thousands of conferences held all over the world that need speakers. They want to provide their attendees with keynote speakers and presenters that stand out. Whatever your profession is, you're going to make a splash at an industry conference if you have a book. They will be more likely to invite you to be a keynote speaker or a breakout session leader.

Further still, if you have a book and get some speaking gigs under your belt you might be able to join a speakers agency where they list you as a PAID speaker.

More Clients

Obviously having a book, publicity, speaking gigs and Google Love is going to get you more clients. It doesn't matter whether you're looking for local clients or national clients. You're an expert once you have a book. The more people hear about you and the more credible your business is perceived, the more clients will seek out your services.

Higher Rates

Once you've established yourself as the #1 expert and influencer in your field—because you have this book—you can increase your rates.

I have a client who wrote a lovely memoir—*Out of the Blue: a Psychic's Memoir*—about her life and how her psychic abilities have helped herself and those around her. It's a fun book because it's a romance novel; a truly profound book about passing from life to death; and a very relatable book because it's the story of her life.

This client does psychic readings as her profession. The minute she had a book to put on her table at holistic fairs she was able to double her prices. As soon as she put the book on her website her business doubled and so did her prices; her income quadrupled.

If you're a coach—or any other type of professional—you can charge a premium for your services once you have a book.

Selling at Events

It would be a shame to give a fabulous keynote speech at a conference and not have a book to sell at the back of the room. It wouldn't be smart to go to a networking event and pay for a table without something to sell at the table.

This can be a significant source of sales. The best thing is that you can order the books at wholesale cost and sell them for retail costs, skipping the expense of distribution.

Investment Return

As you can see, a book can BE your marketing. You may not make a million dollars on book *sales,* but you'll make your money back as more clients come to you and you are able to charge a premium for your services.

Tax Write-Off

Because this is a marketing expense, let's not forget about the golden tax write-off. Every single dime you spend— going on retreat, hiring a writing coach, hiring editors, ghostwriters, proofreaders, publishers, designers, marketers, social media pros—it's all tax deductible.

Imagine: you go on a writers' retreat on the Mayan Riviera in Mexico. The flight, accommodations, food, retreat cost, transportation— all of it is tax deductible.

You then hire a company like mine, Sioux Ink, and every bit of the editing, design and administration is tax deductible.

After that, all the marketing to get the book out there is tax deductible.

Once the book is out there your income increases as a result of being a published author. AND it's all tax deducible.

How is this not the most brilliant decision you've ever made?

> Writing is an exploration.
> You start from nothing
> and learn as you go.
> ~ E. L. Doctorow, Novelist

STEP 1: RESEARCH

The first step in writing a book is research. This is where you conceive of an idea and then allow it to grow inside of you.

So many people think of this phase as daunting and overwhelming. They believe it's a time-consuming slog, rather than an effortless creative process.

While there are many kinds of books which take extensive scientific research, yours probably won't. Textbooks, technical writing for science careers, medical books with studies and evidence to back up claims, law books, and other genres like these will take an extensive amount of research prior to writing the book. It will also take a significant amount of fact checking and re-researching during the editing phase.

But, you've already done far more research than you believe.

Let's take writing a book to establish credibility in your profession as the first example.

You understand your profession. You already know the ins and outs of it. You might still be learning along the way but things change so fast in our modern tech world I challenge you to find anyone who isn't learning their profession on an ongoing basis.

Still, you understand your industry more than, let's say 90% of people who are not in your profession. Add to that your better understanding of the nuances of your profession, perhaps better than 80% of your colleagues.

So there's your research. You've been doing it all along. You've been practicing your craft, accumulating all the knowledge you need to write this book.

Your personal experience in the profession, the stories of your clients; these become more important than facts and statistics because it allows your reader to relate and engage.

If you need to check a fact, hey, that can be done in the editing phase.

If you're writing a book about the history of your family, it's a safe assumption that you've been researching and doing genealogy for long enough that you know the story well enough to tell it.

If you're writing a piece of fiction, you've told the story to yourself so many times in your head that you've already done the research.

Perhaps if it's a historical novel you might want to check your dates and customs of the time. Again, this can be done in the editing phase.

Still, writers take liberties and are allowed to create whatever worlds they want when they write a book.

The point here is that most of you have probably already done the research necessary to write the first draft of your book. Whatever research you haven't done can be completed in the editing process.

I only write
when I'm inspired.
Fortunately, I am inspired
at 9 o'clock every morning.
~William Faulkner, novelist

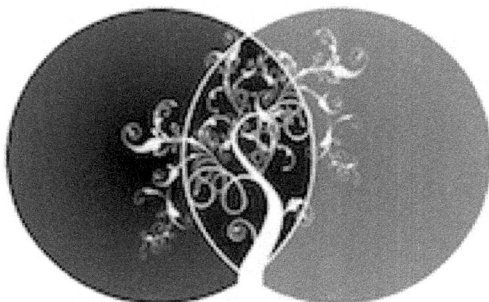

STEP 2: THE ONE THING

It may come as a shock to you, but this step is the *ONLY* STEP <u>YOU</u> HAVE TO DO.

I emphasize this because it's important. When you break the book-making process down into these 5 steps, it becomes clear that there are better qualified, more competent people who can do the other steps for you.

In fact, you don't even have to do this part of the process. Many people, especially experts who need a book for professional credibility, don't even write their own books. They hire professional writers, convey their message and knowledge and step out of the way. It's actually fairly common. I've ghostwritten books and have professional writer friends where all they do is ghostwrite books.

For the context of this book, however, let's say you're going to write your own book.

The one single thing you have to do is get that first draft on paper.

The second half of this book goes into 10 simple ways to accomplish that, so I won't go into greater detail here.

For this chapter I only want you to understand this: you don't have to be overwhelmed because "writing a book" isn't one task. "Writing a book" entails many pieces that others can help you do. Writing a book involves very distinct phases; each of these phases use different skill sets and different expertise.

You can hire people who are really exceptional at their piece of the book-making process. These people will take whatever you have as a first draft and help you make it into something beautiful and readable. They will help you showcase your ideas and thoughts in the best light possible.

You don't even have to be a good writer. Honestly, there isn't a professional writer in the world who should publish their first draft. Unless they want to release a crappy book.

A professional writer would never-ever-in-a-million-years, publish a book without having it professionally edited several times, professionally designed and formatted and gone through multiple proofs.

Why is this lengthy editing process important?

Because books are sacred and to respect them, we owe them—and the reader—the best book we can put out there.

The writer must be
true to truth.
~Thomas Man,
Tonio Kröger

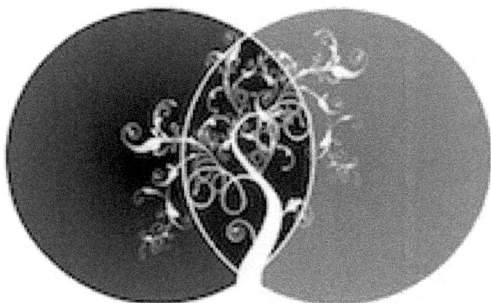

STEP 3: EDITING & DESIGN

Never will I ever put a piece of writing out there that hasn't been professionally edited and designed. Neither should you.

There isn't a single professional writer who would put a book into the world, which hasn't had an editor and a proofreader get their hands on it.

Some writers need less editing; some writers need more. It's irrelevant how much editing your book needs, but it's fundamentally crucial that you do it.

Now, if you feel like you're a not-good-enough writer this should give you great relief. Because a good professional editor can take a so-so book or even a disorganized, poorly written book and spin magic into it.

An editor's job is to make your work as readable as possible.

Professional design is another part of this process and yes, it's a requirement.

Remember that old maxim, "Never judge a book by its cover?"

That's an absurd notion.

Every reader judges a book by its cover, its interior formatting and its marketing. That's all design. They have nothing else to go on.

You should not feel like you need to be a design expert if, in fact, you're not. You should not cheap out and make a generic template on Canva. You should not buy a $5 cover from fiverr.

The only thing a reader has to judge your book on is its cover. Until they've read it.

This means the cover has to be as professional and appealing as possible.

The other piece of design is your interior. White space is an enormously important element in book-making. Consider how you would feel if a book you're reading doesn't have margins or paragraph breaks. It would make the book unreadable. You would be unable to rest your brain where it needs to rest so that you can focus on the concepts being described.

Consider also how font choices and chapter headers can impact a reader's enjoyment of the book.

I'm reading a book right now by one of my favorite authors, and it's a topic that I'm interested in. I've gotta tell you that it's so gaudy in its interior design that it's distracting. The subject breaks are particularly annoying with tacky fish and baseball caps.

Honestly, it makes him look less credible even though the content is good. If I hadn't read several books previously written by him, I would think he's a hack based on the interior and exterior design.

I wrote a book about raising girls a number of years ago. It had a theme about how detrimental Disney Princess story lines are. My designer was able to incorporate that theme into the design of the book using Disney-like fonts on the cover and in the interior. It made the book so much better than if I had used a generic Helvetica or Times font.

Again, these are things you don't have to become an expert in. You don't have to know any of it. All you need to do is understand the importance of it and hire someone who can make your book the best one it can be.

The art of writing is
the art of discovering
what you believe.
~Gustave Flaubert

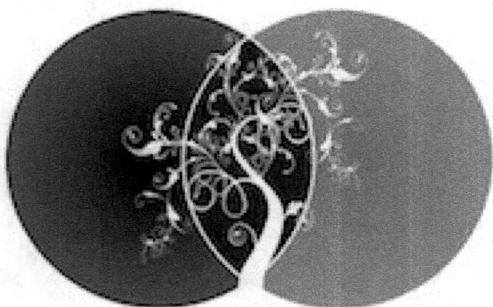

STEP 4: PUBLISHING

There are many, many ways to publish a book in today's marketplace. I've done them all. I have a community of writers who have experimented with the many options as well. I've been able to track results.

The book industry is changing FAST. It changes every day. This started with the Internet Revolution which allows anyone access to authoring—and publishing—a book.

For hundreds of years, this had been a closed process that didn't change. You found an agent, they found a publisher, you sold away your rights and you really didn't have other options. This was mainly because printing books was expensive that few authors had access to it.

That's no longer true today.

I want to share some of today's options with you. I'll share some pros and cons, just so you have a better picture of what's available to you as an author.

Traditional Publishing

Traditional publishing really hasn't changed since the invention of the printing press. Essentially, a publisher finds a book they believe can sell and they buy the copyright to the book, print it and distribute it. Boom. This used to be the only option for authors because it was a heady investment and the average Jane didn't have access to the resources. This is no longer the case.

Cons:

- It takes an average of 18 months from the time you sign a publishing contract to get a book on the shelves. With today's instant Internet tech I can't understand why this would be. But, it is.

- Traditional publishing is on the decline and it has been since the Internet Revolution.

- It's time-consuming and expensive to get a publisher to take on your book.

- You sell your copyright to the publisher. This means they own the content of the book. You no longer own your baby and have no rights to it.

- You have to find an agent and share 20% of your profits with them. This could take *years*.

- The agent has to find a publisher to take the book on. Again, this could take years.

- The royalties per book sold are between 25 and 50 cents per book, which means you have to sell a LOT of books.

- You have to pay the publisher to give you your own book. They own it, after all.

- They control the content. If you write a great book, but they don't think it's marketable, your contract will allow them to force you to follow their instructions for marketability. Otherwise they can dissolve the contract. In the end, you could end up with a book that you don't even like.

- Authors must establish a marketing platform before an agent or publisher will even look at your book. This means you already have to have a social media platform with 5,000 likes on your biz page and 5,000 friends. You have to be established on Twitter, Instagram, etc. They'll want to know about engagement on your newsletter list. Basically, they want to know that you can sell books to a built-in audience.

- Establishing a marketing platform before you even get someone to look at your book is expensive and takes time. You've already made an investment of thousands of dollars and hours before your book can be sold.

- Authors now pay for and do their own marketing. Even after a publisher picks up your book, you'll be expected to pay for your own FB ads, social media campaigns, book tours, and other marketing strategies.

- Once you've paid the publisher their commission, the agent their commission and

rolled out a self-paid-for marketing cam-
paign, you're most likely losing money.

- Traditional publishers have the right, as
part of the contract, to print as many books
as they want. They can also print as *few*
books as they want. If your book doesn't
sell a first printing of say, 1,000 books in the
first few weeks, they can stop printing the
book. You have no say in this.

- The publisher also has the right to position
the book however they like. For instance,
they may decide that they want the book on
a front table at Barnes & Noble, but in two
weeks it's not doing as well as they like, so
it ends up on the shelf with only the spine
showing. Or they just stop distributing it.

- Even after a traditional publisher takes your
book off the market, you still don't own
your copyright. So you'll have to buy your
copyright back if you want to keep it in cir-
culation.

- Generally, you won't be able to buy your
book back for a few years, if at all.

- You'll probably spend a great deal of money.

Pros

- Traditional publishers have established distribution channels to really push your book —if they want to.

- If you grew up in an era of traditional publishing this might be your Big Childhood Dream. You get to have your book *chosen,* and dang, that's gotta feel good.

- Being published by a well-known traditional publisher is a huge ego boost! It carries prestige and cachet.

- You have a knowledge bank of real experts who can help your book succeed.

- Your book will be professionally edited, proofed and designed as part of the package deal. (Of course, remember that you'll have to have the book edited prior to sending it to them or they'll believe it's crap).

- The reach of distribution might increase the likelihood that lightning will strike and you'll make the New York Times Bestseller list. It's a long shot, but sometimes lightning strikes.

Self-Publishing

Cons

- Self-published books are often crap. Which means that people don't want to buy them.

- There are self-publishing platforms out there which offer services like editing, but they're really not involved in the creative process. "Editing" for places like Balboa Press means "proofreading." These are expensive services that do not deliver. They will take a spin through the book, correct some grammar and that's that. You can ask them for two edits. True editing involves a collaborative creative process between editor and writer to achieve the best book possible.

- With these services, you don't even getting contact with the editor. You have a "project manager" who often changes during your publishing process because of high turnover within the company. The project manager is the go-between, never allowing you access to the person actually doing the work.

- Design is the same issue. You can spend a lot of money for a book designer and they will give you two cover choices. Take it or leave it. Again, you get two spins for changes and you only have contact with your project manager, not the actual designer. These covers are created with generic templates, which means there will be nothing distinctive about them to make them stand out on Amazon or on the shelf.

- There is a lot of misleading advertising out there. You might think that Hay House really will read and pick up your book if you self-publish through Balboa Press. You'll pay a steep premium for this hope. At best, it's a long shot. At worse, it's sketchy business practice that leads nowhere.

- Bookstores are unlikely to carry self-published books. Very unlikely.

- Self-published books often languish in Amazon oblivion. They are rarely featured in "other books you want to buy" advertising near similar books in your genre.

- Again, selling a self-published book means that you are going to establish the platform (social media, newsletter lists, blog followers) for yourself.

- You're paying for editing and design no matter what with this approach. Which, is as it should be, frankly, because otherwise you're disrespecting the art, craft and profession of writing by putting out a substandard book. There's no way around it. *Everyone pays for their own dream. Everyone.*

Pros

- The Internet Revolution is what really gave the average Joe true freedom of speech.

- No longer do you have to wait to be *chosen* to publish a book.

- You don't have to write those hideous book proposals to attract agents and publishers.

- You don't have to follow outdated strict rules about submissions. For instance, publishers want to be the *only* publishing house you're trying to sell your book to. Imagine year after year, sending your book out and having to wait for a "no" before you can send it to another publisher. Publishing houses believe it is their "right" to take months to look at your work and send you a rejection letter. Absurd. Unbelievably arrogant.

- You can get a self-published book out quite quickly. With CreateSpace, Kindle and Ingram Spark you can upload a book, whether print or electronic,. in a matter of minutes and get the thing published within a week.

- It's cheap. When you self-publish, you're publishing on-demand (I hope). Therefore there's no huge expense of having 5,000 books printed, which will likely end up in your garage gathering dust.

- You get a higher royalty, sometimes up to 70% of each sale on Kindle or Amazon.

Hybrid Model

Cons

- There are many hybrid models being invented and experimented with. This is awesome! However, it's also a risk.

- There are so many different approaches to innovative publishing that it can be confusing and overwhelming. See the above examples of CreateSpace and Balboa Press services. You're paying a lot of money, but getting little in return.

- Many of these companies haven't been established long. This is because they are innovators and trail-blazers in a burgeoning and ever-changing industry.

- From company to company there is no industry-established standard. So you'll want to look at your contract carefully.

- While distribution channels exist for small publishing houses, they aren't as wide as traditional publishers. Yet they are much wider than self-publishers. As these small presses grow and experiment, they'll achieve broader distribution.

- There are upfront costs that any and all authors are going to have to pay. These include professional editing and design, ISBN numbers, marketing, building a platform, etc. There's no way around this, friends. Still, at least a hybrid publisher can handle these elements together to make a cohesive and appealing design.

Pros

- Third-party credibility is critical to establish your book as legitimate, precisely because self-publishing has a bad rap (deserved or not).

- Having a publisher's logo on your book is instant credibility.

- Bookstores are more likely to carry a book with a publishing company imprint.

- Professional editing and design are often included in a publishing package.

- You get what you pay for. Some hybrid publishing companies, including my own, operate on a "services rendered" basis. This means you pay for editing and design, administrating Amazon and Kindle publishing, and use of ISBN numbers. But it's TRUE editing and design with collaboration with editors and designers, not just a project manager.

- You are able to buy your own book at wholesale costs to sell at speeches or trade shows or simply to give away. These costs are based on printing prices determined by the number of pages in the book, the percentage taken by the distributor and the bookseller's commission.

- You own your copyright in some cases. (Make sure you don't sign your copyright away in a hybrid publishing contract.) This means that if you use the content to give freebies on your website, create a course out of the content, get parts of it printed in a magazine or any other use, you have the right to do it. With traditional publishing, I'm sorry, but you have to get their permission to use your own content outside of the book itself.

- You maintain creative control over your work. Hybrid publishing companies, like Sioux Ink, are there to provide a professional service. Of course, any legitimate publisher will want to make sure that the books they publish aligns with the company's brand and values, but they will also grant ultimate creative control to the author. That said, don't be silly, take a professional's advice and follow it. After all, this is what they do. Use the expertise you're paying for.

- You keep the profits. Sorta. Because hybrid companies are operating on shoestrings and bra straps to keep costs down, you're going to have to pay for services upfront. However, you also don't have to pay a bunch of fees or royalties to the publisher when the book begins to sell. Business models are constantly in flux because this is a completely new form of publishing, so you'll have to negotiate with the publisher. Some might want 10% on book sales (which sure beats paying 80% to the publisher), others may not take any royalties at all.

- You have access to a broader network. A hybrid publishing company wants to market itself based on work accomplished. Which means that you'll get access to marketing on a publisher's website, social media, press and any other platform the publisher wants to advertise on. This expands your reach beyond what you've personally established.

Sioux Ink Publishing

My publishing company, Sioux Ink, is a hybrid model. I've published traditionally, on spec for major publishers and I've used CreateSpace services.

I never intended to be a publisher. But, there's a fun story about how Sioux Ink came to be.

I went to a Hay House conference in March of 2014. We did a meditation in one of the workshops, and when I came out of it I looked down at my hand, and there was written *"Tracee Books"* in blue ink. Now, I thought it was funny for me to write my own name on my own palm. And I honestly had no memory of doing it. I chuckled and blew it off.

Later in the same conference, I was participating in another meditation exercise and flow writing in my journal. Coming out of that meditation I looked down at my journal: *"You're going to start a publishing company."*

"Huh. Maybe someday," I thought. I didn't put much stock into it. I was doing other things, like publishing my book *The Year of YES!*, working to build my coaching practice and putting together a mastermind. It simply wasn't on my radar. Starting a publishing company wasn't my dream or ambition.

I had written, "Year of YES! Publisher" on my annual vision board that January. I figured to get my book out I'd need to *find* one. Not BE-COME one.

When I went to publish my book *The Year of YES: What if you said YES! to everything your Soul told you to do in one year?* in I investigated my publishing options anew. I looked at it from a business perspective—would it lead client's to my coaching practice and establish me as a legit author?

I *hated* all of them. I couldn't understand why a traditional publisher couldn't get a book out in under 18 months and I didn't want to wait that long. I was in labor and I needed that book out of me ASAP.

The idea of writing a book proposal made me want to throw up. The idea of chasing agent after agent down—possibly for years—turned my stomach. The further idea of waiting for who knows how long to find a publisher—if ever—exhausted me.

I also wanted to control my own work. I wanted to own it, reuse the content whenever I wanted, own my own copyright, have creative control, be able to position my book to lead to more clients to me and get the most out of my own marketing efforts. I had spent a great deal of time, energy and money on my marketing efforts in the ten years previous.

But, I absolutely did not want the lack of credibility of self-publishing. I'm a professional writer and I'm great at what I do. I don't want to be perceived as putting out unprofessional work. I want professional editing and design and a publisher's logo on my work.

Having published using CreateSpace design and editing services before, and having many conversations with Balboa Press, I didn't want to throw good money down the toilet to end up with an average book with little to no true editing.

The only thing that was hard to let go of for me was that childhood dream of being chosen by a big publisher.

But, Loves, I found my way around that when I understood, from a business perspective, that I wanted the most out of my investment and I wanted to put the best book possible out there.

To continue with the story of how Sioux Ink was born, I found myself registering Sioux Ink with Bowker (the company which issues all U.S. ISBNs) as a publishing imprint.

By November of the same year, I had launched a publishing company. Just like my Soul told me I would.

With no advertising or marketing at all, word got around and authors began coming to me to help them tell their own stories and get their own books published.

How's that for destiny or kismet or whatever you want to call it?

Writing is easy,
all you have to do is
cross out the wrong words.
~Mark Twain

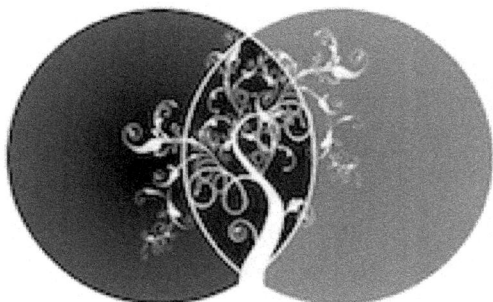

STEP 5: MARKETING

Now that you have a tangible book in your hands, you're so excited. You tell all your friends, you buy 100 books to give everyone a copy. It's a huge achievement and you're so proud. As well you should be!

You envision hundreds of people rushing to buy your book once it goes live on Amazon. You expect every friend and relative to shell out some money, read the book and leave glowing reviews.

At the end of the launch, you've made a few bucks and you're so excited. Yet, after that initial push, you realize that you're selling a book or two a month—if you're lucky.

What gives?

Remember our birth metaphor. You've given birth and now you have a kid to raise. As we all know, raising kids is a marathon, not a sprint. It takes a good long 18 years—full of struggle and learning and joy and fear and persistence—to raise a human being into adulthood.

So it's true with marketing a book.

Marketing is a cumulative process. Before you even have a book to sell, you want to start building a following and letting people know who you are. One way is to friend people on FB and growing your social media contacts through a newsletter list.

Once the book is written and ready to publish you want to do a big push so that people will anticipate it's publication.

Once it's out, you'll have to do a big push to launch it, scrounge reviews, tell as many people as possible, study book marketing and arrange some press to expand your reach.

Then you have to employ persistence and stamina to the book marketing process. If you really want your book to rank on Amazon, if you really want to share your message with as many people as possible, you're going to have to be consistent with marketing it.

This seems daunting, and sometimes it can be. But, once you set up a system it can roll on its own for a while.

Again, there are people who study book marketing and do it for a living. Some of them offer classes teaching you how to do it yourself. Others take over the task and do it for you.

If you don't have a budget, you'll have to figure it out yourself. You just wrote a book! You can learn anything!

Still, time and energy are a huge factors that keep people from marketing their books effectively. Maybe you have a full-time job or kids or other responsibilities. It's likely you simply don't have time to dedicate yourself to giving the book the attention it needs to grow into a healthy adult.

That's OK!

Hiring professionals, even for a short period of time to launch the book and create an automated system is the obvious thing to do. To not do it seems silly considering all you've already invested just to give birth to this thing.

Now you know that the absolute one thing you have to do is to get your thoughts on paper, somehow.

The one thing you must do to write your book is simple: WRITE IT.

So let's look at **10 Easy Ways to Write Your Book**.

The art of writing is
the art of discovering
what you believe.
~Gustave Flaubert

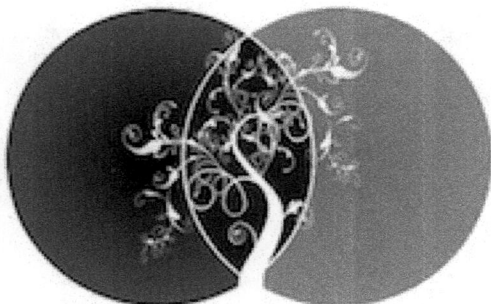

10: GHOSTWRITING

I mentioned ghostwriting your book as a viable option. Experts and professionals do it frequently. You know the latest book you read about that new diet? The doctor probably didn't write it. He was too busy doctoring.

This is excellent because the expert can deliver their knowledge without taking the time or learning the craft of writing. Their knowledge is presented in the best light possible.

Their business increases because a book establishes them as an expert. As an expert they can get on radio shows, podcasts, television shows and be asked to speak at professional conferences.

All without actually writing a book.

Consider this: if you have two lawyers to choose from to handle your estate and one has written a book with valuable information, while the other has a banner at a bus stop—which lawyer would you hire? The one with the book, obviously.

Most books that are ghostwritten are based on interviews the writer has with the professional. They take information and then weave their craft into it.

A major reason to consider a ghostwriter is because you simply do not have time to write the darn thing yourself. That's valid.

One of my clients, Anna Rawlins was working on growing her Airb$b Investor Style business. She knew she needed a book to establish herself as the premier expert in her field. It's a very innovative industry, she understood that providing information to potential property investors would greatly increase her business.

She made an outline and wrote several chapters in her book *Airb$b Investor Style*. It was good. Her bubbly personality came through her writing in a very engaging way.

Then the book languished at the bottom of her to-do list for a year. She'd been pre-marketing the book as an upcoming "release in January." But that was January 2017. Soon it was September 2017 and it hadn't gotten done. To finish it in time for a 2018 launch date, she needed help.

She gave the book to me; we did several interviews about what she wanted the book to accomplish for her. She shared with me the content she wanted to include in the book about her industry.

I wrote the rest of the book for her, maintaining her unique voice and vision. The only thing she had to do was approve the book, asking for any changes she felt appropriate.

Easy Peasy.

Write like a
motherfucker!
~Cheryl Strayed, author

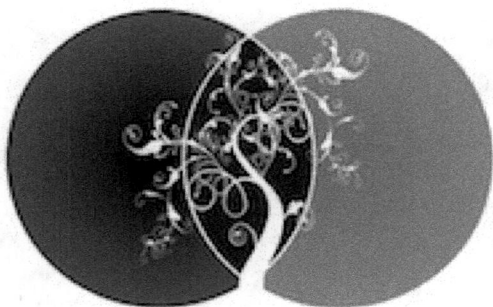

9: CALENDARIZE IT

Commonly, writers set aside time for book writing just as they would any of their other responsibilities.

In my calendar I have kickboxing every Monday at lunch and every Friday morning. I know that it needs to be on my calendar so that I don't double book myself and end up missing my fitness time. I do this because I prioritize maintaining my fitness and health. I know that if I don't have it on the calendar I might schedule a meeting or get distracted and do something else.

The same method can be used for writing. Maybe you write daily. Perhaps you write once a week. You'll have to look at your calendar and find a spot to squeeze it in.

Here's the thing: most of us are so dang busy and distracted that it's almost impossible to find a bunch of random hours in which you're able to truly focus on writing.

This is not to say that you can't make it happen. Most professional writers have an established schedule. They wake up in the morning and do the same thing everyday: write.

"I only write when I'm inspired, I make sure that I'm inspired every day at 9 am," is a famous quote about the productivity of writing. This quote has been attributed to countless writers, it's difficult to say who said it first.

I know people with full-time jobs who sacrifice sleep, waking at 4 am to get their writing done first thing, before anything can distract them.

I, personally, do not recommend sacrificing sleep because of the value it provides to your creativity and productivity. But, if that's what you've gotta do, you gotta do it.

Start writing,
no matter what.
The water does not flow
until the faucet
is turned on.
~Louis L'Amour

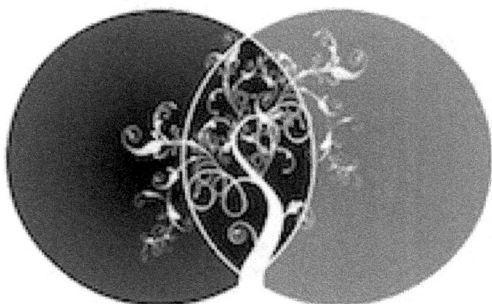

8: PIECE BY PIECE

I had a client who had a book in her. She knew her subject and had a lot of great information to share with people. But, good heavens she was daunted by the task.

I knew she was never going to do it unless we broke it down into achievable pieces and then made a book out of it later.

I encouraged her to create an online course in her field and sell it online as a one-year program. Each month she would write 11 short emails with great information and send them to subscribers. She did this for one year.

By the end of the year, she had 200,000 words which we made into a year-long journey in book form. I gotta tell ya, recording the audio version of that book was a major feat! That's a lot of content and we spent weeks in my recording studio (re: walk-in closet).

The point is, we were able to break the task down over a year-long period, making it less daunting. The reason it was different than simply calendarizing writing, is that it was an entirely separate product while it was being created. While being created she was selling these "chapters" as a monthly subscription for $11 a month. This may not seem like a lot of money, but it adds up if you get enough people to sign up.

It was also a great motivator to keep her on track with the writing. Because people were expecting what they paid for, she didn't find distractions and excuses to put the writing off. She simply held up her end of the bargain, which was to write her audience an email.

Then we made a book.

When I wrote *The Girl Revolution Manifesto* I broke it into 13 chapters and then committed to writing one chapter a day. It worked. I then committed to editing it one chapter a day. I had small kiddos at the time, so that was the best I could do. But, that book happened. It was written at the end of 13 days.

Some writers break it down to number of words per day, others break it down to number of hours or minutes per day.

Break it down to whatever feels less intimidating to you. Also, don't set goals that you'll be unable to accomplish. Be realistic about your time and energy, so that you're not constantly disappointed in yourself.

The pen is
mightier
than the sword.
~Edward Bulwer-Lytton

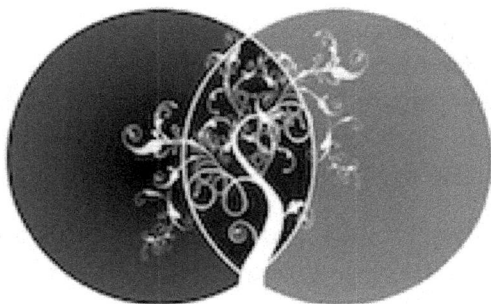

7. REPURPOSE; REPACKAGE

In the early 2000s, I had an advocacy website called "The Girl Revolution" where I wrote about issues facing girls in our media-saturated culture. I covered everything from early puberty to media messages to Disney princesses to parenting strategies to domestic violence to beauty ideas and so much more. By the end of my five-year project I had over 1,000 blog posts on my website.

Two things happened over the years. One, I published a book which was simply a compilation of related blogs. I went through the content already created on my website and put it into book form.

Two, I wrote a manifesto of everything I had learned through research and interviews. *The Girl Revolution Manifesto* was a great book that I didn't have the guts to publish. I had a not-so-secret fear of Mean Girls on the Internet. It kept me from publishing my work for a long time.

Flash forward from 2009 to 2016 and this book still pestered me from my desktop. It took up my mindshare. It hijacked my creative energy. It made me feel like a loser for not just publishing the darn thing.

I finally pulled the book out just to get rid of it! I wanted to stop thinking about it and feeling guilty about it. Of course, after sitting on my desktop for seven years, some things had changed.

We had gone from George W. Bush to eight lovely Obama years and now Trump was president. If you don't understand the gender issues involved in those major leadership changes you're missing a lot.

Also, my daughter was a little girl when I began The Girl Revolution project. I had stopped doing that work when she went to middle school because I knew it was time to stop talking about her in public. In 2016 this daughter—my muse—was a freshman in high school. So basically, all of my theories about parenting and specifically about parenting girls had demonstrated either that they worked or that they hadn't.

I had new perspectives on issues and new ideas about how to handle them and I had this brave, strong daughter as an example of how my ideas really DO work.

What I was focusing on in my writing had also changed. In 2009 there was more fear and anger in my work. In 2016, I had started living a different way—intuitively listening to my inner voice. I had also begun parenting a different way.

In 2009 it still felt like there was a formula for success in America. By 2016 I understood that all formulas were crumbling and the best thing we can teach our children is to trust themselves to figure things out as they come up.

I realized that this manifesto of mine needed an additional book. I wrote 11 extra chapters and packaged them with the original book. It's a fascinating experiment because you can see the growth pattern.

So, ask yourself what you can repurpose and repackage to make a book. Maybe you have a blog, or teach classes and can combine the curriculum into a book or workbook, perhaps you've written poetry or children's stories over the years which can be made into a book. Maybe there are travel journals sitting in your closet waiting for their day.

There is validity to repurposing information for different audiences and readers.

The scariest moment
is always just
before you start.
After that, things can
only get better.
~Steven King, On Writing

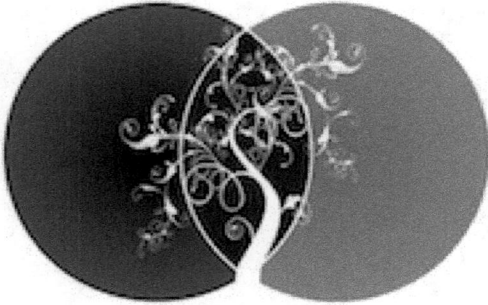

6: NaNoWriMo

Deadlines are the bomb! Many people don't finish books because there is no deadline. Which means you can get distracted and procrastinate until ... someday ... when you have more time and aren't so busy.

The problem with that strategy is that in our modern world there will never be a moment when you have more time and aren't so busy.

A book-writing challenge with a clear deadline could be the turning point for getting the book written.

NoNoWriMo is short for National Novel Writing Month. It's an annual book writing challenge, taking place every November, in which authors commit to finishing an entire book in 30 days.

For some, this is exactly the push they need. But, not for as many as you might think. Out of the 200,000+ people who participated in 2016, only 20,000 completed the challenge. That's only a 10% success rate.

In order to understand the world, one has to turn away from it on occasion.
~Albert Camus,
The Myth of Sisyphus

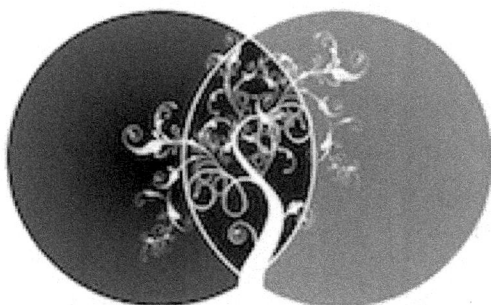

5: SABBATICAL

To write a book, you have to create space for it in your life. Some people are able to finagle sabbaticals or foundational grants to complete a book.

For instance, if you're in education, you could talk to your university and work out a semester or two off to focus on writing a research book.

Some writers can apply for grants and fellowships, which will pay them a stipend so that they can take time off work to finish their book.

Good for them. Most of us don't have that luxury.

More realistic for most of us is if we can convince our significant other to take the financial load for a time so that we can pursue our dream.

Some people quit their jobs and live off their 401k and credit card.

Others look for ways to make money passively so that they can devote themselves to the work.

Personally, I take a month in a warm climate every February because I can telecommute. Sometimes I have tons of creative energy and can write a book, other times I'm so exhausted from my everyday life, the best I can do is rest enough to rev up for the next leg of my journey.

Because book writing requires focus and charged up creativity, look for ways to take a sabbatical. Look for ways you can finance some time off. Look for opportunities which allow you to telecommute and work around your writing schedule.

When we sit down each day and do our work, power concentrates around us. The Muse takes note of our dedication. She approves. We have earned favor in her sight. When we sit down and work, we become like a magnetized rod that attracts iron filings. Ideas come. Insights accrete.

~Steven Pressfield,
The War of Art

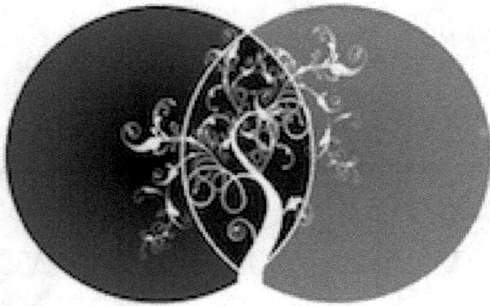

4: COMPILE

I have this friend, Joanne Bamberger. She's a political pundit who is dedicated to bringing a variety of women's voices and perspectives together. So, she writes books that include other women's essays.

In other words, she doesn't have to write the whole book. She writes her part and then extends the opportunity to other writers to contribute.

Not only does this take some of the burden off of her, she's able to use the platforms and marketing reach of all the other writers to aid in the success of the book.

Perhaps you have a network of people who are interested in the same things you are. Maybe you don't write the whole book. Instead, you collect other people's work and incorporate it into a single book.

Let's say you're a certified nutritionist and your goal is to inform people about how they can maintain health through food.

But, you understand that one program isn't right for every person's body and metabolism. Now let's say that you're very into being vegan. But, you understand that realistically, many people aren't going to want to be vegan.

What you might do is invite other nutritionists to write about their particular expertise in the book. You get a ketogenic specialist, a paleo expert, someone who knows a lot about the microbiome and someone who has expertise in diabetic nutrition.

Now you have a book which helps people understand the difference between several different ways of eating in one place so that they can compare easily.

You also have several other contributors who want that book to sell as much as you do.

They too will be using their marketing platforms to market the book.

So who gets the proceeds? I guess you can work that out with the contributors. However, I will say that when I contributed to Joanne's book *PunditMom's Mothers of Intention: How Women & Social Media Are Revolutionizing Politics in America*, I didn't make a penny and I was fine with that.

If people don't like what you're creating, just smile at them and tell them sweetly to go make their own fucking art.
~Elizabeth Gilbert,
Big Magic

3: SPEAK NOW

People communicate in different ways. They feel confident with one method over another. For instance, my friend Darryl loves to market his business with video. He's great at it; he feels confident that he's getting his message across.

Some people are simply more verbal. They do better when they can hear their words spoken versus when they have to write them down.

Who says you can't make a book that way?

No one.

One of my authors realized this about herself. She was crunched for time and didn't want to sit at a computer. Her business is real estate and she needed to continue to hustle doing her actual job. She knew she needed the book for credibility, but she also acknowledged that speaking her knowledge would be a faster, easier way for her to convey her knowledge and ideas.

She recorded what she wanted to share in a recording app on her phone. Each topic—mortgages, insurance, investments—had its own recording.

She then submitted those files to a transcriber. The transcriber returned the recording in a text document.

Then I made a book out of it. I was able to take her knowledge, organize it in a way that made sense to the reader and fill out the book with transitions.

Another client was working on a crime thriller. He is a natural oral storyteller. So he wrote down his story in a first draft. Then he had the Microsoft robot read the book back to him so that he could understand how it sounded, making changes along the way. It helped him get clear on the book as a whole.

To be vulnerable—to really
put yourself out there,
and lean into it—is to
live courageously.
~Dr. Brené Brown,
The Power of Vulnerability

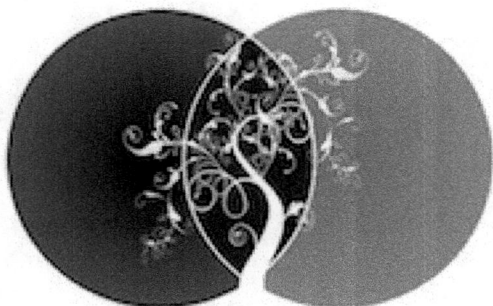

2: FOCUS & FLOW

You're simply not going to write a book unless you can focus on the writing of it.

This isn't your fault. Think about the last time you were able to truly focus on one single thing. Focus without your to-do list running through your head, without text and email and phone calls bombarding you, focus without checking your social media, focus without worrying about global warming or the climate, focus without replaying that conversation with your boss over and over in your head.

I bet it's been a long time— if it's ever happened at all.

This isn't a problem that just you have. This is a problem we ALL have. From the time we wake until we shut our eyes, we're accosted with media and other people's demands on our attention in every aspect of our lives from getting the kids to school to driving down the street to checking our email. Advertising, media, marketing, 24-hr news, fake news, ads posing as news, newsletters, social media envy, commercials, event invitations, texts from people we love and people we don't love.

Who can focus? Our attention spans are such that we can't even watch a seven minute video to learn something we need, or even desire, to learn. We sign up for online classes which promise to fix our problems, but can't even focus long enough to finish the course.

Still, you're not going to write a book unless you find a way to focus.

In fact, you're not even going to be able to hear the sweet melody of the book's voice if you can't find enough silence to focus on it.

It's hard, my friends. But, if this is important to you, you're going to have to do it.

Fractured Focus = Fractured Results.

If this is a thing you want to finish, you'll have to find some strategy to go off the grid for a while. Remove yourself from the extreme flood of information we're subjected to daily to give your book the attention it deserves.

Think of it this way. If you're nearing the last few weeks of your pregnancy what are you going to focus on? You're going to make space and time to be able to focus on this monumental undertaking. You're going to make sure you have your work caught up and you have the support you'll need to take care of this baby. You're going to find a doctor or doula to help you when the time comes. You're going to clear your schedule so that you have time to care for a newborn. You'll make sure the nursery is ready and your space is soothing and relaxing.

Your book is the same way. It needs this type of focus for it to be welcomed into the world.

Once you've made space to focus, it's time to get into "flow".

Flow is a state of consciousness which we can enter to allow books to come to us rather than us chasing them down and slogging through.

To reach a flow state a person must be simultaneously challenged and experiencing pleasure. Not so challenged as to cause discomfort, but challenged enough to stay engaged and focused.

Writing isn't torture, it's not arduous and it's not overwhelming when you are doing it in flow. When people say they want to write a book but they hate writing, I know they are *doing it wrong*. Writing in a flow state is the most pleasurable experience I know.

Flow is something you've experienced before; almost everyone has. It may not have happened while writing, but flow is universal to various activities. It's the reason we keep doing what we do.

I've heard software developers describe writing code in a flow state; painters, dancers, skiers, runners, business strategists, inventors, surgeons, teachers, parents, hikers, cops, robbers ... everyone can reach a flow state.

You'll know you're in a flow state when what you're doing involves such focus that you lose time. You'll know that you've achieved it when you're experiencing such pleasure that you don't want to stop.

Remember sitting in school and looking at the clock thinking, "Oh God, there's still 45 minutes left?!?!" and experiencing gut-wrenching despair?

Flow is the opposite of that. Flow is when you look at the clock and realize that you have to stop doing what you're doing and you feel a little sad. You want to keep doing it because it feels so *good*. But, you have to go get the kids or make dinner or meet that friend for a drink.

When you write in flow, you're not going to want to stop. So many brilliant books are born through flow.

Flow is my favorite way to write a book. You can try various methods to reach flow, but below is a book meditation to get you started.

Some writers might call this free writing. You may worry that this is a difficult process but it shouldn't be. You don't have to be gifted or be an experienced meditator to do it.

The meditation process is really about freedom and being able to let go. Just write. Let the words come how they want to come. Let them be what they want to be.

Just like a ballplayer might have rituals before a game, a writer can incorporate rituals to prepare themselves for writing. One of these rituals can be meditation. Try the following meditation to see if it works for you.

How do you know if it works? Well, were you able to let go and allow the words to come without judging them as good or bad? Then it worked. Did you enjoy the process? Then it worked. Did you get words on paper? Then it worked.

The awesome thing about book meditation is that you'll get better at it as you practice it. You'll train your brain and body quickly to relax and enter the meditative state. You'll eventually go deeper, more effortlessly than you could when you started.

Book Meditation

Close your eyes and just take a few relaxing breaths deep into your abdomen. Take a moment to feel the breath move in and out with consciousness and awareness.

Feel your feet ground into the floor. Imagine roots growing out the bottoms of your feet deep into the center of the earth, holding you steady, tethering you to the Earth realm, even as you prepare to travel into a creative state of consciousness.

Call on your highest self to silence all of the outside voices that distract you from your creative inspiration. Your Ego must be silent, your mother's voice must be silent, Oprah's voice must be silent, your church, parents, culture, media, politics and all other outside voices must be silent.

Now invite the creative inspiration within you to speak.

Your highest self is now invited to write anything that it feels needs to be written. You may also ask direct questions. Be open to any word, phrase or sentence. Write down any feelings, thoughts or impressions. Record any knowings or inklings that come to you.

Do not question what comes to you or demand to know the meaning during this exercise. It's not your job to "figure it out," right now. Your only job is to listen and be open to whatever words, phrases, images, smells or colors that come.

You will not judge this gift or dismiss it. You will welcome all communication offered, knowing that there is meaning in it for you and your book.

Visions, images, smells, sounds, scenes from media, colors and all other impressions are all welcome.

Please begin to write and don't stop until your Soul is complete.

Obviously, this is YOUR meditation so choose whatever words, spiritual traditions and rituals that work for you.

Want to write a book?
Get out of your own life!
You're not so important
that the world can't live
without you for a week.
~Tracee Sioux, Sioux Ink

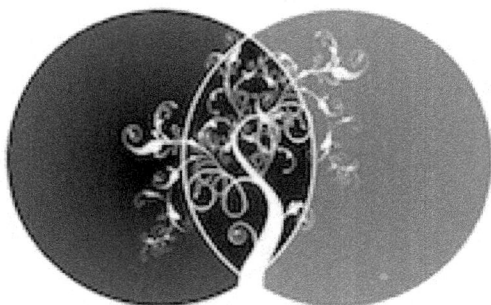

1: RETREAT

The #1 way to write a book is to go on retreat.

GET OUT OF YOUR OWN LIFE!

This is always how I have to do it. (Well, except for that first draft of writing *The Girl Revolution Manifesto*, when I had a toddler climbing all over me—and I gotta tell you, that was HARD.)

We've talked about the hardship of filtering through the cacophony of information we're swimming through all day, every day; the responsibilities and demands of other people; the time and energy constraints of getting a book written when you're holding down a job and trying to fulfill other responsibilities; we've talked about the danger of being available for texts, social media, emails, alerts and your own over-full and exhausting calendar; we've talked about how difficult it is to focus and reach a state of flow while you're swamped with your own daily life.

A writing retreat solves all of these issues.

I want you to think about this: **When was the last time you focused on only one thing?**

If you really think about it, the answer could very well be *never*.

But, to write a book, that's what you need. To focus only on that one thing.

In 2015 I had a book whispering to me. It wanted to be written and I wanted to write it. But, my life was my life, just like yours is; busy, chaotic, full, sometimes overwhelming.

I got an email from a writers group I belonged to inviting me to a writing retreat. Two days, a weekend. It was months away, but I signed up thinking I'd get to work on that book that wanted to be born.

Through that year this book would tug at me and I would tell it, "I'm busy now, I'll focus on you in November."

November came and I showed up to that retreat with a title *Soul vs. Ego Smackdown: How to say YES! to your Soul and tell your Ego to Suck It*, and a vague idea of a format. I had told this book to hush while I lived my life and hush it did. So, I didn't know anything else about the content of this book.

The first day we sat in a group and outlined our intentions for the weekend. I said, "I'm going to write a book." A tall order when everyone else is making goals like finishing three chapters or writing 5,000 words.

I opened the blank document and started writing as fast as my fingers could type. The words were coming so quickly and effortlessly that I could barely keep up. I would read the words on the page as they were written and think "Oh, I didn't know that's how this worked."

I couldn't recognize the ideas, because I'd never formulated them before.

I was 100% in flow. The words were coming through me without a conscious thought process.

We quit at 5 pm for dinner and started again in the morning. The same flurry of writing happened for me the second day.

As the last day wound to an end, so did my 35,000-word book. I had channeled an extreme amount of creative energy in a very short period of time and I could feel my very cells vibrating so fast that I didn't even know what to do with it.

They were calling me for a group picture as I closed my laptop; I rushed to be in the photo, mere minutes after finishing the book.

I kid you not, in that photo there is a halo around my head. You can see the light energy around me.

Believe what you will about that experience, but I know this—it felt fucking phenomenal. It was the most sublime, exquisite experience I've ever had.

I want this for you.

To get this experience, you're going to have to get out of your own life and retreat from the burdens of living. You're going to have to focus and allow yourself to get into a creative space that you've never experienced before.

There are lots of writing retreats out there. The trouble with most of them is that they aren't a space for writing, they're about learning about writing.

You don't need to know about writing. You need to write.

You need to write in a different place from where you live. An inspiring place. Maybe the beach or the mountains. I've taken myself on retreat in both places. I even took myself to a Buddhist retreat center and simply focused on my work in a spiritual environment.

It does not matter how well you write, whether you have a 100% formulated book in your head ready to go on paper, or whether you're writing fiction, non-fiction, memoir or any other genre.

What matters is that you create the space for the book to be born.

When I take writers on my **Book Smackdown Sanctuary: Write Your Book in One Week** retreats, it's to an exotic location. Travel itself makes us more present and focused. Traveling to an exotic location like the Yucatan Jungle inspires creativity simply because it's not that same tree outside your office window.

I take writers for *one single week* to focus on one single task. Most people have never focused on one single thing for an entire seven days. They are skeptical that a book can be written in such a short amount of time. There's a lot of writing folklore about laboring over a book for years and years, but that's totally unnecessary. I know this because I've ghostwritten books in 13 hours, and this book itself was written in one workday. I've helped other people do the same. (Please note that it's only the writing which takes so little time when you're focused and in flow; there is still much work to be done with editing, design, proofreading and marketing.)

When you focus on one single thing for a short period of time you're going to be shocked and awed about the miracles that can be performed.

The time factor in a one week retreat is very powerful too because there is a firm deadline. Do it. Don't dink around. Focus. There is an expectation of a clear accomplishment that must be done within a specific time frame. A gorgeous deadline.

An exotic location also provides ample opportunity to rest and play. Here's what I know from a lifetime of creativity: rest and play are essential. When you have time to sleep and linger in a hammock, you're allowing your body to enter into a state of consciousness much like the state of flow we discussed. When you allow yourself to experience pleasures like swimming in the ocean, eating different foods and experiencing different cultures, you're opening a whole new portal of creativity. So many more ideas will come compared to the ideas you'll have in your own neighborhood.

There's also a very important community energy component to a retreat. Obviously, sometimes a solitary retreat can be just the thing. But, there is also a collected energy created by groups of people dedicated to the same activity. When you're in a room with 12 people who are all writing in a state of flow and exchanging ideas you're going to absorb all of that creative energy and it's going to spark all kinds of new ideas!

My retreats are working retreats. There's information, but essentially, the idea is that you create the space and information so that you can get that first draft done!

Remember the 5 Steps to Writing a Book? We're doing ONE of those steps at my retreats. We're writing a first draft.

Here's the thing about first drafts: no one will ever see them. This allows you to let go of self-consciousness and doubt because it doesn't even have to be "good." It just has to happen. It's sooo freeing to tell yourself, "This is only for me." It claims the pleasure of the process as your own, as well as releasing the pressure of having to do it perfectly the first time.

There isn't a professional writer in the world who would ever publish a first draft. No, after that draft is written there is ample time to edit, reorganize, rewrite, research, fact check, and proofread. In fact, you'd be a fool if you didn't do these things.

But, at a Book Smackdown Sanctuary, for one week of your life, you get to focus on the single, pleasurable task of writing that first draft.

It's a life-changer for your personal growth and can be a game-changer for your career.

You just have to make the time and space for it.

Are you ready to Write Now?

You write for yourself.
You publish for others.
~Tracee Sioux, Sioux Ink

TOO BUSY TO WRITE?

Visit this link for an exclusive FREE Course.

https://mailchi.mp/traceesioux.com/time-joy-gasm

You can also find me on Facebook at www.facebook/traceesioux and www.facebook.com/Yes-TraceeSioux

ACKNOWLEDGEMENTS

I have an amazing community which helps me survive and thrive both personally and professionally. These are people who not only support me in crisis, but cheer my success and push me forward. It's easy to support someone when things are bad, but your true tribe celebrates your success even more than you do.

The best of my tribe include Ainsley and Zack, my two kiddos.

I'm all atwitter about Jean-Paul and I bow to whatever forces that *finally* allowed us to find and keep each other. (Universe, you better not take this as a dare to ruin our blooming romance!)

To my brilliant conspirators in my personal and professional life, I don't know how I would do life without you. Some of these include: Anna Rawlins, my BFF fellow traveler; Christina Verg, who keeps me looking pretty and young, as well as being a cherished friend; CJ McDaniel, who keeps my psychic energy in check; Sarah Dille, without whom I couldn't balance parenting and profession with any sanity whatsoever; and Darryl Stewart, who meets me in Mexico every February, rescuing me from going bonkersville nutzballs in the Colorado winter.

Thanks to my Facebook friends. As a professional who works from home, you're my water cooler and a fabulous source of learning and connection.

Thanks to Sarah Saint-Laurent for being my book promoter and Kasie Clark for doing the final proofreading of this book.

A special thank you to all of my authors who are brave enough to put themselves out there with their beautiful stories and brilliant ideas. I am honored to use my craft to serve you.

I'm profoundly grateful for the written word; my playground, my craft, my challenge, and the longest love affair of my life (so far). This craft has kept me captivated and has allowed me to be a force for creativity and light. The well never runs dry.

To every editor, client and author who has influenced me much thanks for allowing me the opportunity to learn and dive deep into the ocean of writing, editing and publishing.

My Soul, my inner wise woman, thank you for never letting me quit this profession—

which I've often wanted to turn my back on when it just gets so hard! From Journalist to Publisher, the industry changes so fast it's enough to spin my head, and at times has made me broke as fuck. I don't like that. So Creative Geniuses, it's time to bring prosperity as a reward for using my gifts, always persisting and being a badass motherfucka at this craft.

And thank you, dear reader. Without a reader, a writer's purpose is only half fulfilled.

ABOUT THE AUTHOR

Tracee Sioux is the owner of
Sioux Ink Publishing

She is the author of over a dozen books including, *The Year of YES!* and *Soul vs. Ego
Smackdown: How to say YES! to Your Soul and
Tell Your Ego to Suck It!* Sioux lives in Colorado
with her two children. www.traceesioux.com

Sioux Ink is an innovative full-service publishing company. With our complete packages we charge an honest fee, with no hidden costs, and take zero of your profits. Zero. You keep your copyright and your creative control. We believe authors are the stars of content.

Services offered include:

* Ghostwriting
* Editing
* Cover Design
* Interior Design
* Distribution Administration
* ISBN & Registration

www.siouxink.com